*To my three best friends, Erik, Emma, and Wyatt, with love.*
—H. M.


*For Henry, Charlotte, and Ike—*
*May all your "play dates" with each other and your friends*
*be filled with joy and happiness.*
*With love,*
—L. R.

What to Expect at a Play Date
Text and illustrations copyright © 2001 by Heidi Murkoff
What to Expect Kids® is a registered trademark of Heidi Murkoff.
Growing Up Just Got Easier™, and Angus™ are trademarks of Heidi Murkoff.
HarperCollins®, 📖®, and HarperFestival® are registered trademarks of HarperCollins Publishers Inc.
Printed in the U.S.A. All rights reserved.
Library of Congress catalog card number: 00-108645
www.harperchildrens.com

# What to Expect
# at a Play Date

## Heidi Murkoff
## Illustrated by Laura Rader

HarperFestival®
A Division of HarperCollinsPublishers

# A Word to Parents

**R**emember the ear-to-ear grin on your child's face the first time he or she spied another baby in a nearby stroller? From very early on, children are social creatures. But, as any parent who's served as referee/mediator/activity director at a preschool play date (and has taken enough aspirin to tell about it) can attest, children start having play dates long before they are socially *skilled* creatures.

To young children, who have developed a strong sense of self but are just beginning to get a sense of those around them, a play date presents many challenges—from sharing to taking turns to dealing with disagreements. It also presents a wonderful opportunity to start learning the social skills they'll need to succeed in school, at work, and in all of their future relationships.

Whether your child is a newcomer to play dates or has been on the circuit for some time, there are plenty of ways you can help nurture the development of those all-important social skills. *What to Expect at a Play Date* is a good place to start. It will answer many of the questions your child may have about the logistics of play dates (who you have them with, where you have them, what you do at them). But this book will also explain the benefits of sharing, of taking turns, and of generally "playing nicely" at a play date—which, while obvious to parents, may be mystifying to the typically egocentric three-year-old. It will tackle, too, some of the thornier issues children (and their parents and caregivers) confront at play dates—what to do if a friend doesn't share or take turns, how to respond if a friend does something decidedly unfriendly (such as grab a toy or hit), how to leave a play date gracefully (in other words, without a tantrum). And because today's play dates can groom your child for tomorrow's dinner parties, issues of etiquette are also addressed—from the proper

protocol for a "guest" and a "host" of a play date to follow, to the polite way to ask for help when you can't quite get your pants back on after a trip to the potty.

Many of the activities in *What to Expect at a Play Date* (marked by a paw print on each page) are devoted to what could best be described as "discussion questions." These are meant to get your child thinking, but also to get the two of you talking—and to give you the opportunity to share insights accumulated in your comparatively vast social experience. For instance, you might talk to your child about things you do to make a friend happy, or ways of expressing frustration and anger that work for you and are socially acceptable.

Of course, while the success of a play date does depend somewhat on the cooperation of the play daters, there are many strategies parents and caregivers can use to help ensure (relative) harmony. Among these strategies are to time play dates well—not only so they're shorter and thus sweeter, but also so they don't coincide with naps; to plan some adult-directed activities—so when the joys of cooperation wear thin you can step in with a collage project that pleases everyone; and to schedule a snack—hungry children are cranky children.

You'll notice that I have help explaining to your child what to expect on a play date. Because learning should be fun, too, I've created Angus, a lovable dog who provides answers to questions about growing up. Angus serves as a best friend and confidante throughout all of the What to Expect Kids® books. He's a "transitional object" who will hold your child's hand as he or she faces new— and sometimes challenging—experiences.

For many more tips on how to make play dates more fun for you and your child, read *What to Expect the Toddler Years*.

Wishing you many enjoyable play dates. . . .

*heidi*

There are so many ways you can have fun on a play date.

# Just Ask Angus

**H**ello! My name is Angus. Some people call me the Answer Dog, because I like to answer all kinds of questions about growing up. It's good to ask questions because what you know, helps you grow!

So, I hear you're going to have a play date. Maybe it's the first play date you've ever had, or maybe it's the first time you're having a play date with a new friend. Either way, I bet you're going to have fun!

Do you know what a friend is? A friend is someone you like to spend time with. A friend can be a boy or a girl, someone who's older or someone who's younger, or someone who's exactly the same age as you. A friend can be someone you've met at day care, someone who lives in your neighborhood, or someone you've met at the playground or a gym class. But most important of all, a friend is someone who's fun to play with!

Even if you've had play dates before, I'm sure you still have lots of questions. I'm here to help—just ask me!

Are you ready to find out what to expect when you go on a play date? Then let's get started! Follow me. . . .

Your friend,
**Angus**

P.S. I've put a little game or idea to think about on the bottom of every page. Look for my paw print, and you'll find it! Have fun!

# What's a play date?

A play date is a special visit with a friend, a time for the two of you to play together and have fun. Some play dates will be at your house and some will be at your friend's house. When a play date is at your house, you are the host. When a play date is at your friend's house, you are the guest. Sometimes you may have play dates at another place you and your friend both like to go to, like the playground or the museum. Going places like that is always more fun when you have a friend along!

**Can you think of someone you'd like to have a play date with?**

# Who will be at the play date?

There are two people who will always be at a play date: you and your friend. Sometimes you may even have a play date with more than one friend. If you or your friend have brothers or sisters, they may be at the play date, too. There will also always be at least one grown-up at a play date—usually a mommy, a daddy, or a babysitter. Sometimes your mommy or daddy or babysitter will stay with you while you play at a friend's house. Other times, especially after you've had a lot of play dates, you may get dropped off and picked up, just like you would at school or day care. That's okay, because your friend's mommy or daddy or babysitter will take good care of both of you while you're playing!

Pets can be good friends, too!

**Pet-iquette**
- Always ask before you pet.
- Be gentle.
- No tail or ear pulling!

Angus

Some of your friends may have pets at their houses. Just like people, dogs and cats need to get used to someone new. What are some things you should do when you meet a pet for the first time?

# What will I do at the play date?

At play dates, you get to play, play, play! Maybe you and your friend will build a block castle together (two people can make a block castle that's two times as big!). Maybe you'll play school (you can take turns being the teacher). Maybe a grown-up will help you finger paint or make cookies. Or maybe you'll go to the playground and swing on the swings or slide down the slide together. Another thing you'll do at a play date is share. If the play date is at your house, you will share your toys with your friend. If the play date is at your friend's house, your friend will share his or her toys with you.

**What toys do you like to play with when you're by yourself? Which toys are more fun to play with when you are with a friend?**

Sometimes it's fun to play by yourself.

# Why do I have to share my toys?

Sharing is an important part of being a good friend—and it makes playing together much more fun. Let's say you and your friend want to play teddy-bear hospital. If you share your teddy bears, you'll be able to make a bigger hospital with more patients—and both you and your friend will be able to be doctors! Sometimes sharing is hard, especially sharing your favorite toys. But remember, when you share your toy with a friend, it's still your toy. You'll get it back when your friend is finished playing with it.

Now, can you think of some toys that would be really fun to share?

If you have a very special toy you'd rather not share with your friend, ask your mommy or daddy or babysitter to put that toy away *before* your friend comes over. (But remember, you won't be able to play with that toy either until after the play date is finished.)

# Why do I have to take turns?

Taking turns makes play dates fairer for everyone—and more fun for everyone, too! Imagine you are at your friend's house, and there is only one doll stroller that you both want to use. If you take turns with the stroller, you and your friend will both have a chance to play with it—which means you'll both have more fun! Like sharing, taking turns can be hard. Just remember this, after your friend has a turn playing with a toy, it will be your turn to play next! If you and your friend have trouble figuring out when it's time to switch turns, you can ask a grown-up to help by setting a timer.

**Taking turns is something everyone has to do every day. Can you think of some things that people have to wait their turn for?**

It will be your turn next!

# What if my friend doesn't share?

Everybody has trouble sharing once in a while (even you, I bet!). Sometimes you may have a play date with a friend who's having trouble sharing. If that happens, the best thing to do is to show your friend how nice it is to share. You can do that by giving your friend one of your toys to play with. That may help your friend want to share, too. But if it doesn't, don't get mad. Like everything that's a little hard to do at first, sharing gets easier when you practice. The more you and your friend play together, the easier sharing will become.

**There are some things that belong to everybody and that we all need to share. Can you think of some of these things?**

We all share swings at the playground. What else do we share?

# What if my friend does something I don't like?

**P**laying with a friend at a play date can be lots and lots of fun. But once in a while even a good friend may do something you don't like, like grab a toy or hit or call you a mean name. When a friend does something like that, you should use words to tell him or her how you feel. You can say, "Please don't do that. I don't like it." If talking to your friend doesn't work, you can always ask a grown-up for help. (Hitting back or calling your friend a mean name doesn't help and it's not nice, either.) Sometimes you might be the person who does something that isn't nice. When that happens you should say "I'm sorry" to your friend. Then you can go back to playing nicely again!

**When you do something that isn't nice, a friend can feel bad. What can you do to make a friend feel better?**

A big hug makes me happy!

# What if my friend and I don't want to do the same thing?

Usually at a play date you and your friend will want to play the same game at the same time. But sometimes you and your friend may not agree about what game to play. When that happens there are two things you can do, and both of them are fair. One is to take turns deciding what to do—that way you both get a turn picking out the game. Two is to play different things for a while. (It's fine for you to play different things at the same play date—you're still friends if you do that!) Then later on, if you both want to, you can pick a game you want to play together!

My favorite game is catch!

What are your favorite games to play with a friend? Have a grown-up help you make a list so you'll have some ideas ready when your friend comes over.

# What if I'm hungry or have to go to the bathroom at a friend's house?

**E**very house has food to eat, drinks to drink, and a bathroom to use. When you're hungry or thirsty, or need to go to the bathroom, all you have to do is ask the grown-up who's taking care of you and your friend to help you. That grown-up is also there to help you with anything else you need, like washing your hands before snack, getting the sand out of your shoes when you come back from the playground, buttoning your overalls after you go the bathroom, even fixing a broken wheel on your truck. All you have to do is ask—but remember, always say "please" and "thank you"!

**When you're the host you can show your guest where your room is, where the bathroom is, and where the kitchen is. Practice by taking me on a tour now!**

# When will the play date be over?

Usually the grown-ups will decide when it's time for the play date to be over. Some play dates will be shorter, and some will be longer. Sometimes you'll be glad when a play date is over (you may be tired or you may feel like playing by yourself again). But most of the time you'll probably be a little sad when a play date is over, because you've been having so much fun. If the play date is at your friend's house, you may also be sad that you have to leave all of his or her toys behind. And if the play date is at your house, your friend may be sad to leave your toys behind! If you are sad, the best things to do are to think about how much fun you had and to remember that you'll have another play date again soon!

Cleaning up is more fun together!

One way to be a good guest is to help clean up after the play date. Another way is to thank your hosts when you leave. And if you're the host, you can thank your guests for coming over.